Best Kids
Jewish Holiday
Jokes
EVER!

HA! HA! HA! HA!

Highlights Press
Honesdale, Pennsylvania

Cover Art by Brian Michael Weaver
Contributing illustrators: Jim Bradshaw, Lee Cosgrove, David Coulson,
Jack Desrocher, Keith Frawley, Peter Grosshauser, Dave Horowitz,
Kelly Kennedy, Pat Lewis, Bob Ostrom, Jim Paillot, Rich Powell, Kevin Rechin,
Rico Schacherl, Diana Schoenbrun, Asher Schwartz, Rick Stromoski, Gary Swift,
Betty C. Tang, Jack Viant, Brian Michael Weaver, Pete Whitehead

For assistance in the preparation of this book, the editors would like to thank
Rabbi Judy Greenberg, Senior Jewish Educator at Hillel at the University of
Wisconsin-Madison and Sydnie Ciment, Director of Early Childhood Education,
Temple Sinai.

For information about permission to reprint selections from this book,
please contact permissions@highlights.com.

Published by Highlights Press
815 Church Street
Honesdale, Pennsylvania 18431

ISBN: 978-1-64472-843-7
Library of Congress Control Number: 2022933826
Printed in United States

First edition
Visit our website at Highlights.com.
10 9 8 7 6 5 4 3 2 1

CONTENTS

HANUKKAH HILARITY

Knock, knock.

Who's there?

Noah.

Noah who?

Noah good Hanukkah joke?

What did the loaf of bread say to the other loaf of bread during Hanukkah?

"Happy challah-days!"

What is a llama's favorite holiday?

Llama-kkah

How do runners wish each other happy holidays?

"Jog Sameach!"

What happened when the man took the train home for Hanukkah?

His mom made him bring it back.

Knock, knock.

Who's there?

Festival.

Festival who?

Festival, you should open this door!

Why was the broom
late for work after the
Hanukkah party?

It over-swept.

Sarah: Let me guess what you had for
Hanukkah dinner. You had latkes and brisket.

Micah: Wow! That's amazing. Did you read
my mind?

Sarah: No, your chin.

What's the difference
between Hanukkah and
a dragon?

*One lasts for eight
nights, and the other
sometimes ate knights.*

What came after the first Hanukkah?

The second one

What do you get when you cross Hanukkah with an airplane?

The Festival of Flights

What is a chicken's favorite holiday?

Hen-ukkah

What did the stamp say to the Hanukkah card?

"Stick with me, and we'll go places."

What did the challah do on Hanukkah?

It loafed around.

What's the best instrument to play on Hanukkah?

Harmon-ukkah

What do you get when you cross Hanukkah with an octopus?

Not sure, but 64 of something!

Where does Hanukkah come before Sukkot?

In the dictionary

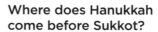

What's a kitten's favorite holiday?

Hanuk-cat

Teacher: Judy, what is your favorite holiday?

Judy: Hanukkah.

Teacher: Spell it, please.

Judy: Oh, I changed my mind. I like Purim better.

What smells the best at a Hanukkah dinner?

Your nose

Knock, knock.

Who's there?

Meyer.

Meyer who?

Meyer Hanukkah be bright and joyful!

How do amphibians
wish each other happy
holidays?

"Frog Sameach!"

Joseph: What are you going to give your girlfriend for Hanukkah?

Ariel: I don't know. She wants something with diamonds on it.

Joseph: How about a deck of cards?

Knock, knock.

Who's there?

Honey.

Honey who?

Honey-kkah is coming!

Teacher: *Hanukkah* is a tricky word. Do you know how to spell it?

Adele: Yes. I-T.

Knock, knock.

Who's there?

Doughnut.

Doughnut who?

Doughnut open this until Hanukkah.

What is a clock's favorite Hanukkah gift?

The present

Mom: Did you thank Ms. Rubin for hosting Hanukkah?

Beth: No, Mom. The girls leaving before me thanked her, and Ms. Rubin said, "Don't mention it." So I didn't.

Teacher: What did the Maccabees do at the first Hanukkah?

Lily: I don't know. I wasn't invited!

What comes at the end of Hanukkah?

The letter H

MENORAH MANIA

What do you get when you cross a dinosaur and a Hanukkiah?

Menorah-saurus

Which hand is it better to light the menorah with?

Neither. It's best to light it with the shammash.

Knock, knock.

Who's there?

Wick.

Wick who?

Wick way to the synagogue?

Miriam: What brand of candles do you want?

Yael: I want brand-new candles!

What do you call a menorah in armor?

A knight-light

What did the menorah say when it went on stage?

"This is my time to shine."

What did the match say to the candle on the menorah?

"Lighten up!"

What did the candles say when the menorah complained about getting too hot?

"Whoa, a talking menorah!"

What did it say on the outside of the fragile menorah box?

Candle with care

What do you get when you cross a volcano with a menorah?

A lava lamp

What do you call tall menorahs?

High lights

Where is the menorah when the candles go out?

In the dark

Why do we put candles on top of the menorah?

It's too hard to put them on the bottom.

Why did the monster eat the menorah?

It wanted a light snack.

Ava: Someone stole my candles!

Asher: Oh no! Are you annoyed?

Ava: No, I'm delighted.

Where do you find the most famous menorahs?

In the Hall of Flame

Knock, knock.

Who's there?

Olive.

Olive who?

Olive the oil was gone, except for one jar.

How many candles did the menorah eat for lunch?

None, it already eight.

What did the menorah say to the shammash?

Nothing—menorahs can't talk.

Why did the menorah go to school?

It wanted to get brighter.

Dad: What was that loud noise?

Jonathan: The tablecloth fell on the floor.

Dad: Why would the tablecloth falling make such a loud noise?

Jonathan: Because the menorah was on top of it.

Knock, knock.

Who's there?

Delight.

Delight who?

Delight coming from de menorah is beautiful.

Knock, knock.

Who's there?

Shammash.

Shammash who?

Shammash food—we could feed an army!

Which candle burns longer—a blue candle or a white candle?

Neither. They both burn shorter.

Are candles happy or sad when they go out?

They are delighted.

How do you make the candles on a menorah stand up?

Take away their chairs.

Molly: What do Hanukkah candles smell like?

Akim: They don't smell like anything.

Molly: Makes no sense.

Akim: That's right—they make no scents.

When would you have 18 candles at Hanukkah?

When there are two menorahs!

What did one candle say to the other candle?

"Are you going out tonight?"

Teacher: Yoseph, your essay titled "My Menorah" is similar to your brother's. Did you copy his?

Yoseph: No, it's the same menorah.

Knock, knock.

Who's there?

Oil.

Oil who?

Oil be right back.

LATKE LAUGHS

Yaffa: Oh no! My latkes aren't getting crispy.

Bubbe: Don't give up. Just keep on frying.

What do you call leftover latkes?

Later taters

What's the best day to make latkes?

Fry-day

Knock, knock.

Who's there?

Norma Lee.

Norma Lee who?

Norma Lee we eat latkes with sour cream.

What did the latke's mom say when it got embarrassed?

"Fry not to blush."

What do you call a lazy latke?

A couch potato

Why are potatoes such good lookouts?

Because their eyes are peeled

Mom: What's that smell, sweetie?

David: You know how you were worried I'd burn the latkes?

Mom: Yes, I remember.

David: Well, your worries are over.

Who is the most evil potato?

Darth Tater

What did the bubbe say to her family on Hanukkah?

"I love you a latke."

Why didn't the teddy bear want any latkes?

It was already stuffed.

What do you call a stack of latkes?

A balanced meal

What's the difference between a potato and an onion?

No one cries when you cut up a potato.

What does an onion a day do?

It keeps everyone away.

Did you hear about the angry latke?

It just flipped.

What do you need to break in order to use it?

An egg

Eitan: Wanna hear a joke about cutting onions?

Noa: Sure!

Eitan: It'll have you in tears.

What do you call a stolen latke?

A hot potato

Why did the latke cross the road?

It saw a fork up ahead.

Mom: Did you eat all the latkes on the counter?

Tamar: No, I didn't touch one.

Mom: Then why is there only one left?

Tamar: That's the one I didn't touch.

How many potatoes does it take to make a potato pancake?

A latke!

What do you call someone who can't turn latkes?

A flip-flop

Knock, knock.

Who's there?

Harriet.

Harriet who?

Harriet so many latkes he got sick to his stomach.

Why did the potato go to the doctor?

It wasn't peeling well.

Why was the latke a bad singer?

It was too flat.

What do you get when you cross a potato with an elephant?

Mashed potatoes

Kid: I'm excited to learn how to make latkes with you, Bubbe!

Bubbe: Grab those potatoes. We're off to a grate starch.

What do monsters eat with their latkes?

Sour scream

Why did the latke go to France?

It wanted to be a french fry.

What do you call a baby latke?

A small fry

Why did the chef make latkes the week before Hanukkah?

She was frying to save time.

What do you call burnt latkes?

Spud duds

A sweet potato latke gave his mother a gift. As he did, she said to him, "Awww, why are you so sweet?"

He replied, "I guess that's just the way I yam."

Omer: Dad, these latkes taste kind of funny.

Dad: Then why aren't you laughing?

What's the best latke topping?

More latkes

What's the secret to making latkes last?

Make the applesauce first.

Knock, knock.

Who's there?

Howdy.

Howdy who?

Howdy-licious are these latkes?

How are latkes served to astronauts?

On satellite dishes

Robin: Dad, will the latkes be long?

Dad: No, they'll be round.

(Mom and Shoshana are making latkes.)

Mom: Why is there an egg on the front porch and an egg on the back porch?

Shoshana: The recipe says to separate two eggs.

How does a penguin make latkes?

With its flippers

What did the pan say when it was introduced to the latke?

"I'm very pleased to heat you."

Sydnie: What's that thing in the pan with the latkes?

Sloane: It's an unidentified frying object!

Knock, knock.

Who's there?

Latke.

Latke who?

Latke be said about Hanukkah!

FOOD FUNNIES

What did the boy say to the pickle?

"You mean a great dill to me."

Knock, knock.

Who's there?

Challah.

Challah who?

Challah-days are my favorite days of the year.

What did the brisket say when it was wrapped up as leftovers for the third night in a row?

"Drats! Foiled again."

(At dinner)

Ilana: Dad, are bugs good to eat?

Dad: Let's not talk about that at the table.

(After dinner)

Dad: Now, what did you want to ask me?

Ilana: Oh, nothing. There was a locust in your matzo ball soup, but now it's gone.

What did the herring say when he was caught on the fishhook?

"I'll get canned for this!"

Why did the superhero save the pickle?

Because he wanted to eat it later

How did the Jewish onion greet his cousin on Saturday?

"Shallot Shalom."

What did the bubbe say about the messy kitchen?

"This is so dish-appointing."

A woman walked into a deli to order rye bread. The cashier asked, "Would you like your bread cut into six slices or twelve slices?"

The woman replied, "Six, please. My family could never eat twelve."

What did the shark have for lunch?

A corned reef sandwich

What do cucumbers say when they're in trouble?

"I'm in a pickle."

What do you call a fake kugel?

An im-pasta

What does a pickle say when it wants to enter a card game?

"Dill me in."

Why did the jelly roll?

Because it saw the apple turnover

Why can't a jelly doughnut drive a car?

Because it would get into a traffic jam

Which kind of bagel can fly?

A plane bagel

GRRRRRR

What are two things you can't have for Hanukkah dinner?

Breakfast and lunch

Why are challah jokes always funny?

Because they never get mold

Knock, knock.

Who's there?

Nosh.

Nosh who?

Nosh on my watch!

What is Hanukkah dinner's favorite sport?

Brisket-ball

Where does brisket keep its business papers?

In a beef-case.

What did the pot say to the borscht?

"You're soup-er!"

What's better than a good friend?

A good friend with sufganiyot

Why did the pickle go to the doctor?

It felt dill.

When do basketball players love sufganiyot?

When they dunk them

Why did the baker make some challah?

She kneaded a snack.

Why was the bagel so upset?

It was schmear-itated.

What do you call a selfless pastrami?

Pastram-you

How can you tell a clock is hungry?

It goes back four seconds.

Why did the sufganiyah have a guitar?

It liked to jam.

What kind of bagel is a grandfather's favorite?

Poppy seed

Where does brisket go for vacation?

The Great Barrier Beef

What gets served at many meals but is never eaten?

The guests

Which instrument plays only sour notes?

The pickle-o

Ms. Weiss: Can you please bring me what the lady at the next table is having?

Waiter: Sorry, ma'am, but I'm pretty sure she wants to eat it herself.

What do baseball and sufganiyot have in common?

They both need the batter.

Why did the sufganiyah go to the dentist?

To get a jelly filling

How do you keep a bagel from getting away?

You put lox on it.

Why didn't the moon want any brisket?

It was already full.

What's the best thing to put into a sufganiyah?

Your teeth

Knock, knock.

Who's there?

Schmear.

Schmear who?

Schmear's looking at you, kid.

A man goes into a deli. He's in a rush to get home to light candles for Hanukkah. He says, "Get me a chocolate babka, and step on it!" So the deli clerk gets babka and steps on it.

What kind of game does lox like to play?

Salmon Says

What do you get when you cross an alligator with a pickle?

A croco-dill

What do you call a powdered doughnut on a windy day?

A doughnut

What's green and makes holes?

A drill pickle

Knock, knock.

Who's there?

Dish.

Dish who?

Dish is a delicious meal!

Ruth: Mom, I have jelly on my face.

Mom: Well, wash it off. You're already sweet enough without it.

Benjamin: Oma, how long did it take you to make this brisket?

Oma: Only nana-seconds.

(Chaos breaks out during a trial.)

Judge: Order! Order in the courtroom!

Mr. Hoffman: A pastrami on rye, please.

Dalia: I have a super-secret recipe for babka.

Yoni: What is it?

Dalia: I can't tell you. It's on a knead-to-dough basis.

Jonah: How do you like the matzo ball soup I made?

Sadie: It's soup-endous!

> Knock, knock.
>
> *Who's there?*
>
> Nova.
>
> *Nova who?*
>
> Nova way this is the same lox we have at Savta's!

Mrs. Benowitz: Hello, police? Please send an officer to 324 Pine Street right away!

Hal: Sorry, this isn't the police station. It's Hal's Delicatessen.

Mrs. Benowitz: Oh. In that case, please send over a pastrami sandwich.

Knock, knock.

Who's there?

Pickle.

Pickle who?

Pickle little flower for your mother.

Knock, knock.

Who's there?

Tel Aviv.

Tel Aviv who?

Tel Aviv it's time for dinner!

Talia: Do you eat with your right hand or your left hand?

Roni: Neither. I eat with my fork.

Teacher: You have ten sufganiyot. You eat eight of them. What do you have now?

Asa: A stomachache.

Hannah: Do you know who invented kugel?

Julia: No, but I bet he used his noodle.

Shira: Waiter, is there any matzo ball soup on the menu?

Waiter: No. I just wiped it off.

DIZZY DREIDELS

What did the dreidel say to the menorah?

"Spin too long since we saw each other."

What did the farmer sing on Hanukkah?

"Dreidel, dreidel, dreidel, I made it out of hay."

Knock, knock.

Who's there?

Gimel.

Gimel who?

Gimel all your gelt!

Knock, knock.

Who's there?

Hey.

Hey who?

Hey, I get half the pot!

Knock, knock.

Who's there?

Nun.

Nun who?

Nun for you!

Knock, knock.

Who's there?

Shin.

Shin who?

Shin, shin, put one in!

What is a dreidel's favorite vegetable?

Spinach

You have ten pieces of gelt in your pocket and you lose five. What do you have in your pocket?

A hole

Why did the dreidel go to the doctor?

It kept getting dizzy spells.

What is a chef's favorite Hanukkah song?

"The Ladle Song"

What did the car say to the dreidel?

"Want to go for a spin?"

How did the kid feel after he ate all the chocolate?

A bit gelt-y

What did the dreidel say at the audition?

"Gimel a chance to show you how I roll!"

Teacher: Sophie, if I gave you two pieces of gelt and Avi gave you four pieces of gelt, how many would you have?

Sophie: Eleven.

Teacher: Incorrect. You'd have six.

Sophie: But I already won five pieces of gelt in the last round!

Teacher: Jordan, if I gave you three pieces of gelt and Meira gave you two pieces of gelt, how many would you have?

Jordan: Zero.

Teacher: No, you'd have five.

Jordan: But Meira always eats all her gelt!

What do you get when you cross gelt and a car?

A coin-vertible

What type of dreidel does an octopus play with?

A dr-eight-el

What has a head and tail, but no body?

A chocolate coin

What do you get when you cross a ladybug and a dreidel?

A ladle

What do you call a spinning potato?

A rotate-o

Why is gelt never on time?

Because it's chocolate

How can you get rich by eating?

Eat gelt.

What's the surest way to double your Hanukkah money?

Fold it.

Turnip #1: I'm really sad. I lost my dreidel.

Turnip #2: Don't worry, it will turnip soon.

Why did the dreidel buy a car?

So it could go for a spin.

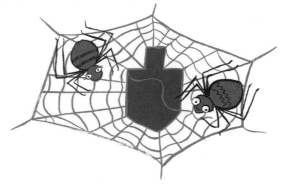

Why are spiders the best at the dreidel game?

They know how to spin.

Why did the boy put his Hanukkah money in the freezer?

He wanted cold hard cash.

Why didn't the lobster share his gelt?

He was shellfish.

Why did the dreidel made out of clay not work?

It got fired.

What's the absolute best Hanukkah present?

A broken drum—you can't beat it!

Where are dreidels made?

O-clay-homa

How much Hanukkah gelt did the little skunk get?

One scent

Which side of the dreidel gives you the most gelt?

The outside

What did one dreidel say to the other?

"See you around!"

MACCABEE MIRTH

What did Judah eat at the first Hanukkah?

Mac-and-cheese-abees

Why did the spotted cat get disqualified from the Maccabiah Games?

It was a cheetah.

Who was the smartest man in the Torah?

Abraham. He knew a Lot.

What did the Maccabee say to the menorah?

"You light up my life."

Which Maccabee wore the biggest yarmulke?

The one with the biggest head

Which Maccabee could jump higher than a temple?

All of them—temples can't jump.

Who invented fractions?

Antiochus the 1/4th

What can't the strongest man in the world hold for a quarter of an hour?

His breath

How many Maccabees does it take to change a light bulb?

What's a light bulb?

Where did Judah keep his armies?

In his sleevies

Why did the Maccabee say "knock, knock"?

Because he was in the wrong joke

Why is it so hot in the stadium after the Maccabiah Games are over?

Because all of the fans have left

What do you call a sneezing Jewish soldier?

Macca-sneeze

There were eight Maccabees huddling under an umbrella. The umbrella was only two feet in diameter. No one got wet. How is that possible?

It wasn't raining.

What is the most popular sport at the Maccabiah Games?

Jew-jitsu

Goldie: What's the difference between a Maccabee and a macaroon?

Dinah: I don't know. What?

Goldie: Remind me not to send you to the grocery store!

How many men were born in the second century BCE?

No men were born— only babies.

Where was Solomon's Temple located?

On the side of his head

What is Judah's favorite vegetable?

Macca-beets

Who was the greatest comedian in the Bible?

Samson. He brought the house down.

Teacher: Can you name five Maccabees in ten seconds?

Rebekkah: Sure. Judah and the other four.

Why is basketball the messiest sport at the Maccabiah Games?

The players dribble all over the court.

What is Judah's favorite singer?

Maccabee-yoncé

Knock, knock.

Who's there?

Jon.

Jon who?

Jon me for dinner?

What did the confused Maccabee say?

"To Maccabee or not to Maccabee!"

How did the Maccabees sleep in the Temple?

With their eyes shut

How do you stop the Greek army from charging?

Unplug it.

Teacher: For homework tonight, I want you to write an essay on Judah Maccabee.

Charlie: I'd rather write on paper.

What kind of music did the Maccabees like?

Rock of Ages

Knock, knock.

Who's there?

Simon.

Simon who?

Simon the other side of the door. If you opened up, you'd see!

FAMILY ANTICS

Knock, knock.

Who's there?

Ari.

Ari who?

Ari there yet?

Uncle Malachi: How was your Hanukkah, Joel?

Joel: Great! We had Bubbe for dinner!

If you eat two-thirds of a babka, what do you have?

An angry mom

What does it mean when you come into the house and you don't have any chores?

You're in the wrong house.

Which family had the biggest seder?

It's all relative.

A woman is going to visit her parents for Hanukkah. She walks into a railroad station and asks the ticket agent, "May I have a round-trip ticket, please?"

The ticket agent asks, "Where to?"

And the woman answers, "Back here again, of course!"

Gigi: You should eat some spinach. It will put color in your cheeks.

Keturah: Who wants green cheeks?

Mom: Lisa, please pick up your room before Oma and Opa get here for Hanukkah dinner.

Lisa: I don't think I'm strong enough.

Knock, knock.

Who's there?

Aunt Lou.

Aunt Lou who?

Aunt Lou do you think you are?

Shuli: Where are you going? Mom said not to walk on the kitchen floor unless your feet are clean.

Eyal: My feet are clean. It's my shoes that are dirty.

(A family of pickles is about to drive across the country to visit relatives.)

Baby Pickle: What if we have car trouble?

Mom Pickle: It'll be OK. We'll just dill with it.

Morgan: I can make you say *purple*.

Erica: No, you can't!

Morgan: OK, say the colors of the Israeli flag.

Erica: Blue and white.

Morgan: That's right.

Erica: But you said you'd make me say *purple*.

Morgan: There, you just said it!

Adina: I just flew in from New York.

Adam: Wow! Your arms must be tired.

Why did the onion go to the other onion's house?

They were having a family re-onion.

Hebrew School Teacher: Do you say prayers before eating?

Jared: No, I don't have to. My dad's a good cook.

Kayla: Mom, I'm glad you named me Kayla.

Mom: Why?

Kayla: Because that's what everyone calls me.

Jacob: Mom asked you to fix Hanukkah dinner.

Elijah: Why? Is it broken?

Caleb: Happy Hanukkah, Tata!

Tata: Why did you give me a bunch of scrap paper?

Caleb: Because I love you to pieces!

Knock, knock.

Who's there?

Rabbit.

Rabbit who?

Rabbit carefully—it's a present for my mom.

Mrs. Katz: My son came to visit for Hanukkah.

Mrs. Cohen: How nice. Did you meet him at the airport?

Mrs. Katz: Goodness, no. I've known him for years!

Mom: Dinner's ready! Oh, wait. We need glasses.

Eliana: I don't need glasses. I already have a pair.

Mom: What are you doing?

Jude: I'm washing my hands.

Mom: Without soap and water?

Jude: Haven't you heard of dry cleaning?

Knock, knock.

Who's there?

Leah.

Leah who?

Leah the door unlocked
next time!

Mr. Appelbaum: Do you make life-size
enlargements of photos?

Photo clerk: Yes, that's our specialty.

Mr. Appelbaum: Good! Here are some pictures
of my family at the Western Wall.

Mr. Shulman: The brisket
I was cooking for my
family was going to be a
surprise.

Mr. Finkelstein: What
happened?

Mr. Shulman: The fire
trucks ruined it.

Dad: Why aren't you doing well in Hebrew school?

Lev: Because the teacher keeps asking about things that happened before I was born!

Nadav: I made these socks for my brother at college.

Erez: They're lovely, but why did you knit three socks?

Nadav: In his last letter, he said he'd grown another foot!

Knock, knock.

Who's there?

Sarah.

Sarah who?

Sarah doorbell around here? I'm tired of knocking.

Reuben: My aunt plays the piano by ear.

Ella: Well, my grandpa fiddles with his whiskers.

Sloane: Mommom, can I go out and play?

Mommom: With those awful holes in your socks?

Sloane: No, with the kids next door.

Rachel: Why are you dancing on the gefilte fish jar?

Michael: Because it said *twist to open*.

Ayla: Will you remember me forever?

Dad: Yes!

Ayla: Knock, knock.

Dad: Who's there?

Ayla: I thought you said you'd remember me!

Dad: Would you like a pocket calculator for Hanukkah?

Gavi: No, thanks. I already know how many pockets I have.

PUNNY PASSOVER

What should you not say to matzo on Passover morning?

"Rise and shine."

What did the lion say after tasting the bitter herbs?

"Ma-ROAR!"

What gets served at many meals but never eaten?

Guests

What did the z'roa say before mealtime?

"Bone appetit!"

What did the Egyptian pyramid architects say after frogs fell from the sky?

"Well, now there's more green space."

Why did the Egyptians comb the desert?

Because there were lice

What is the best way to describe Moses and Aaron when the first plague started?

Blood brothers

Teacher: Nadir, can you tell me where the Red Sea is?

Nadir: Yes, it's on the third line of my report card.

What was Aaron's official title?

Chief of Staff

How does Moses make his coffee?

Hebrews it.

What did the Egyptians wear during the second plague?

Open-toad sandals

Who sang at the Passover seder?

Elvis Parsley

Knock, knock.

Who's there?

Israeli.

Israeli who?

Israeli good to see you!

What did the child ask at the seder when his mother set the table with unusual utensils?

"Why is this knife different from all over knives?"

Why do you always find the afikomen in the last place you look?

Because once you've found it, you stop looking

What did the baker say to the matzo?

"I don't knead you."

Why did the matzo quit his job?

Because he didn't get a raise

Two ants were running across a box of matzo ball mix. One stopped and said to the other, "Hey, why are we running so fast?"

"Didn't you read what it says here?" answered the other ant. "Tear across the dotted line!"

Why were the Egyptians happy when the Nile turned to blood?

Because it was B-positive

Where did Moses go when he wanted to exercise with his brother?

He went out for Aa-run.

What did the cowboy take to Passover dinner?

A horseradish

How did the pharaoh enslave the Jews?

He created a pyramid scheme.

Why can't you go more than halfway into the Red Sea?

Because then you'd be going out

Why didn't the pharaoh call for help during the second plague?

He had a frog in his throat.

Why did Moses squeeze Egypt?

He was trying to get the Jews out.

What dessert might have been served in Egypt during the third plague?

Lice cream

How do you drive your mother completely insane on Passover?

It's really a piece of cake.

Who led the Jewish people across a semi-permeable membrane?

Os-Moses

What's the best cheese to eat on Pesach?

Matzo-rella

What is the king of Egypt's favorite side dish?

Farro

Knock, knock.

Who's there?

Elijah.

Elijah who?

Elijah wake at night counting sheep.

What happened when Moses threw a white rock into the Red Sea?

It got wet.

Where's the best place to shop for Passover dinner?

Seder Joe's

Why couldn't anyone make a phone call when the boils struck?

Service was spotty.

How many pharaohs does it take to screw in a light bulb?

One, but he won't let it go.

Why do we have a Haggadah at Passover?

So we can seder right words.

What root vegetable did Moses's sister enjoy eating?

Miri-yams

What are the most appropriate foods to serve on Passover to commemorate the Red Sea miracle?

Split pea soup and a banana split

How is a good sermon like a piece of matzo?

They should both take less than 18 minutes.

Why are gold-colored, knee-high socks forbidden on Passover?

They create golden calves.

What do cars eat on Passover?

Unleaded bread

Knock, knock.

Who's there?

Aaron.

Aaron who?

The Aaron here is a little stuffy. Could you open a window?

Where does the U.S. military store its hametz?

Fort Leavenworth

Why didn't most Egyptians know about the ninth plague?

They were kept in the dark.

Teacher: Naomi, please use the word *denial* in a sentence.

Naomi: Denial is a river in Egypt.

Knock, knock.

Who's there?

Passover.

Passover who?

**Passover that kugel to me, please.
It smells delicious!**

**What is the last thing
an Egyptian would have
ordered for breakfast during
the sixth plague?**

A hard-boiled egg

**What song was sung to the pharaoh during the
seventh plague?**

"Hail to the Chief"

**What is small, red, and
whispers?**

A hoarse-radish

**What kind of cake do you get after the big
Passover meal?**

A stomach-cake

SHAVUOT SILLIES

What type of cheese is the most talkative Shavuot guest?

Chatter cheese

What did Cinderella say when she was waiting for her order?

"Someday my blintze will come."

Why aren't grapes ever lonely?

They always come in bunches.

What did Moses say after smashing the Ten Commandments?

"It's OK. I have a backup in the cloud."

What do frogs say on Shavuot?

"Read it, read it, read it."

Why didn't the physicist like his cheesecake?

Because the quark had a strange flavor

What did one cheesecake say to the other as they were going into the oven?

"I think this is a setup!"

What is a calendar's favorite food?

Dates

What is the most exhausted mountain?

Mount Sigh-nai

How many figs can fit in an empty box?

Just one, because after that, the box isn't empty.

Knock, knock.

Who's there?

Ada.

Ada who?

Ada lotta ice cream on Shavuot.

What do cats eat on Shavuot?

Mice cream

Knock, knock.

Who's there?

Barley.

Barley who?

I can barley wait!

What do you get when you cross Shavuot and a mountain range?

Feast of Peaks

What did the man who ignored the commandments say?

"Ignorance is blintze."

Knock, knock.

Who's there?

Ruth.

Ruth who?

The Ruth of the matter is, Shavuot is my favorite holiday.

Why didn't the raisin go to the dance?

It didn't have a date.

Why did the wheat farmer suddenly decide to plant barley instead?

She was going against the grain.

What is a rock climber's favorite fruit?

Pome-granites

Knock, knock.

Who's there?

Wheat.

Wheat who?

Wheat here, I'll go get
my mom.

Clara: How did your
photo of the barley field
turn out?

Max: Pretty grainy.

Which commandment do baseball players
always break?

Thou shalt not steal.

What did the wheat say to
the barley?

"Rye would you say that?"

Knock, knock.

Who's there?

Olive.

Olive who?

Olive celebrating Shavuot!

Knock, knock.

Who's there?

Hannah.

Hannah who?

Hannah me some of that cheesecake, please. I'm hungry!

Knock, knock.

Who's there?

Dairy.

Dairy who?

Dairy goes. Let's catch him!

Why did the kid put grain under their pillow?

They wanted to have s-wheat dreams.

Orly: I brought you dessert.

Perry: What did you bring?

Orly: Uh . . . chocolate soup.

Perry: Chocolate soup?

Orly: Well, this morning it was ice cream.

Adara: Why does your sister only read in bed?

Ora: She likes to read from cover to cover.

Ellie: Did you hear the joke about Shavuot?

Yona: No.

Ellie: It's legen-dairy!

Yona: Did you hear the other joke about Shavuot?

Ellie: No.

Yona: It's cheesy.

Knock, knock.

Who's there?

Figs.

Figs who?

Figs me a sandwich, please.

A pastrami sandwich walked into a restaurant and said, "May I have a blintze?"

The waiter replied, "Sorry, we don't serve food here."

ROSH HASHA-HA-HA-NAH

What's the difference between a shofar and a *Triceratops*?

A shofar only has one horn.

What is a bee's favorite kind of apple?

Honeycrisp

What do cows say on Rosh Hashanah? ·

"Happy Moo Year."

Knock, knock.

Who's there?

Shofar.

Shofar who?

Shofar, sho good. This is a great holiday!

What's the difference between a shofar and a chauffeur?

A chauffeur blows his horn, and a shofar's horn is blown.

What do you call a pomegranate with wings?

A fruit fly

What is big and gray with a horn?

A rhinoceros playing the shofar

What do you call an apple that plays the shofar?

A tooty fruity

What is it called when apples come tumbling down the supermarket counter?

An apple-lanche

What do cheerleaders say on Rosh Hashanah?

"Happy New Cheer!"

What do you get when you mix a Jewish family with fruit?

Apple Jews

Why is honey hard to find in Boston?

Because there is only one B *in Boston*

What's worse than finding a worm in your apple?

Finding two worms in your apple

How do lizards greet each other on Rosh Hashanah?

"Iguana Tova!"

Why didn't the shofar player get a second audition?

He really blew the first one.

What does Swiss cheese call Rosh Hashanah and Yom Kippur?

High holey days

Why didn't anyone listen to the shofar's advice?

It was full of hot air.

Why was the little apple so excited for Rosh Hashanah?

He was going to see his Granny Smith.

What does a tree do to celebrate Rosh Hashanah?

It turns over a new leaf.

What do Hawaiians call Rosh Hashanah and Yom Kippur?

High hula-days

Knock, knock.

Who's there?

Effie.

Effie who?

Effie'd known you were coming, he'd have baked more honey cake.

Dad: Would you like a pomegranate?

Tziporah: I don't feel like a pomegranate today.

Dad: That's good. You don't look like a pomegranate either.

How do cats bake honey cake?

From scratch

Knock, knock.

Who's there?

Isaac.

Isaac who?

Isaac of knocking, so please let me in!

Dad: Would you like some gefilte fish?

Son: I'm not into gefilte fish.

Dad: No, the gefilte fish goes into you!

Knock, knock.

Who's there?

Honeybee.

Honeybee who?

Honeybee a dear and get me some apples.

Knock, knock.

Who's there?

Jacob.

Jacob who?

Jacob your mind! Do you want to hear another knock-knock joke?

How do you divide 16 apples evenly among 17 people?

Make applesauce.

Tenant: Last night the people upstairs were stomping on the floor until after midnight.

Landlord: Did they wake you up?

Tenant: No. Luckily, I was still awake, practicing my shofar.

Knock, knock.

Who's there?

Apple.

Apple who?

Apple on the door, but it won't open!

If you have five apples in one hand and five jars of honey in the other hand, what do you have?

Big hands

SUKKOT CHUCKLES

What did one lulav say to the other?

Nothing, it just waved.

Zachary: Want to hear a joke about building a sukkah?

Matilda: Sure.

Zachary: Never mind. I'm still working on it.

What did the s'chach say to the sukkah?

"I've got you covered."

What kind of ant builds a sukkah?

A carpenter ant

What did one garland say to the other?

"What are you hanging around for?"

Why didn't the Israelites starve in the desert?

Because of all the sand which is there

Knock, knock.

Who's there?

Aravah.

Aravah who?

Aravah-cationed with Myrtle's family.

What do you call a dinosaur in a sukkah?

Stuck

What do mallards hang up in their sukkot?

Duck-orations

Why was the palm tree lonely?

It didn't have any fronds.

How do you find out the weather during Sukkot?

Look up.

Kibbutznik: I'd be surprised if you got ten pounds of lemons from that tree.

Farmer: So would I. It's an etrog tree.

Zoey: Do you know why that willow is always surrounded by fog?

Dad: I don't know. It's a mist tree to me.

What did the breeze say to the sukkah?

"Just passing through."

Why couldn't dinosaurs build sukkot?

Because Tyrannosaurus wrecks

Where are the best places to build a sukkah?

Myrtle Beach or Palm Beach

What do shoemakers celebrate starting the fifteenth day of Tishrei?

Festival of the Boots

Sam: How did you get that scratch?

Lev: See that branch hanging off the sukkah?

Sam: Yeah.

Lev: Well, I didn't.

What did one wall say to the other wall?

"Meet you at the corner."

Knock, knock.

Who's there?

Grape.

Grape who?

Grape to see you again!

What's the hardest part of Hoshanot?

The ground

What do octopuses use to build a sukkah?

Their tentacles

What time is it when an elephant sits on your sukkah?

Time to build a new one.

How do you build a sukkah in outer space?

You planet

(A nail and a hammer were building a sukkah.)

Nail: How'd I do?

Hammer: You totally nailed it!

What did the green grape say to the purple grape?

"Breathe!"

What is never invited into the sukkah but is always there?

Your shadow

Knock, knock.

Who's there?

Bam.

Bam who?

No, I need bamboo for the roof.

What's a dog's favorite part of Sukkot?

Ruff-ing the sukkah

Mrs. Feldman: I went to the store to buy etrog today, but they didn't have any.

Mrs. Singer: What a fruitless trip!

Knock, knock.

Who's there?

Willow.

Willow who?

Willow listen to another
knock-knock joke?

Shopper: Can I put these decorations on
myself?

Store clerk: You could, but they would look
better on the sukkah.

Knock, knock.

Who's there?

Citron.

Citron who?

Citron down and join us!

TU BISHVAT TEE-HEES

Knock, knock.

Who's there?

Tree.

Tree who?

Tree more days until Tu Bishvat.

Knock, knock.

Who's there?

Carob.

Carob who?

Don't you carob-out me at all?

What do you call three trees together?

A tree-o

What did the tree say when it couldn't solve the puzzle?

"I'm stumped!"

What do you call a tree that isn't a sapling anymore but isn't a full-grown tree yet?

A tree-nager

Which type of tree is most likely to get sick?

A sycamore tree

Why didn't the tree play checkers?

It's a chess-nut.

Which tree gives the best high fives?

A palm tree

Tree #1: Where are you going?

Tree #2: I'm leafing. Goodbye!

What do you call an almond in outer space?

An astro-nut

What is a tree's favorite drink?

Root beer

Lev: I wasn't made to be a gardener.

Lena: What do you grow in your garden?

Lev: Tired.

What is a tree's least favorite month?

Sep-timber

Alexander: Do you want to hear a joke about Tu Bishvat?

Cecilia: Sure.

Alexander: It's tree-mendous!

Knock, knock.

Who's there?

Almond.

Almond who?

Almond the other side of the door.

What do you call a tree covered in glue?

Sticky

What does a tree do when it gets lost?

It re-roots.

Knock, knock.

Who's there?

Garden.

Garden who?

Stop garden the door and let me in!

Zakia: Did you hear the joke about the tree falling down in the forest?

Yair: No.

Zakia: Neither did I.

Daveed: Do you think the sapling I planted is growing well?

Elan: I think it's pine. Oak not intended.

Daveed: Will you please leaf me alone with the tree puns?

PURIM GRINS

Where did the hamantaschen go on vacation?

The Bermuda Triangle

Knock, knock.

Who's there?

Mordechai.

Mordechai who?

Mordechai on your teeth this visit. Make sure you're brushing well!

How does furniture fulfill tzedakah?

It does chair-ity.

How do we know Ahasuerus had an aquarium?

He gave Haman the royal seal.

Why did Queen Esther go to the dentist?

To get a crown

Why does DNA always have a boring Purim costume?

It always wears the same old genes.

What's the point of a hamantasch?

It has three points.

What do you wear when you're eating hamantaschen?

Jammies

Knock, knock.

Who's there?

Esther.

Esther who?

Esther another reading of the Megillah tomorrow?

Why was the kreplach upset?

Its fillings were hurt.

Mom: Seth, how many bowls of kreplach soup have you eaten?

Seth: Just one. I filled it up five times.

How are a yardstick and King Ahasuerus alike?

They're both rulers.

Raccoon: How are you?

Rabbit: Fine, but are you OK?

Raccoon: Yes. Why do you ask?

Rabbit: Because Purim was three months ago, and you're still wearing your mask.

What was Queen Esther's royal gown made of?

Poly-Esther

Ximena: Do you have holes in your costume?

Joshua: No, of course not.

Ximena: Then how do you get your feet in?

What's the difference between a gragger and a Rorschach test?

You use a gragger to blot out a name, and you use a Rorschach test to name a blot.

Ms. Bronfman: Before we start working on our Purim spiel, tell me, who has had any stage experience?

Ira: My leg was in a cast once.

Where's the best place to celebrate Purim?

The Boo-Hamans

What kreplach ingredient is always in trouble?

The meat, because it's always grounded.

How did the grandmother knit a suit of armor for her grandson's costume?

She used steel wool.

Knock, knock.

Who's there?

Adar.

Adar who?

Adar you to play a practical joke for Purim!

Why did the hamantasch see a doctor?

It felt crumb-y.

Why do flowers bloom before Purim?

They want to get their costumes ready.

Dad: Jace, don't eat soup wearing a costume.

Jace: This soup isn't wearing a costume. I am!

What do police officers put in their hamantaschen?

Traffic jam

Abby: That's a pretty cool costume you're wearing.

Zara: You think so? It feels hot.

Mr. Katz: Why did you walk through the middle of the Purim spiel?

Marcus: It's just a stage I'm going through.

Knock, knock.

Who's there?

Vashti.

Vashti who?

Vashti dishes and I'll give you some hamantaschen!

What do mountains dress up as for Purim?

Volcanoes

Where do hamantaschen sleep?

Under cookie sheets

Dan: Did you hear the joke about the kreplach?

Leah: No, but I have a filling it's going to be funny!

What's the best craft supply for making Purim costumes?

Masking tape

> **Mrs. Dafilou:** The synagogue was giving away Purim masks for free.
>
> **Mrs. Ehrlich:** Why?
>
> **Mrs. Dafilou:** There were no strings attached.

Alana: Did you hear the joke about the Purim spiel?

Benji: No.

Alana: It's a play on words.

JUST JOKING

What is good for your soul but not your soles?

Dancing the hora

What happens once in Shevat, twice in Adar, but never in Tishrei?

The letter A

What Jewish song celebrates coffee?

"Java Nagila"

Why did the rabbi cross the temple?

To get to the other siddur

What happens once in Kislev, twice in Elul, but never in Nisan?

The letter L

What did one cat say to the other?

"Meow-zel tov on your Cat Mitzvah!"

Knock, knock.

Who's there?

Kippah.

Kippah who?

Kippah up, we're going to be late for temple!

Teacher: Class, please open your geography books. Who can tell me where Israel is?

Chaya: I know! It's on page 20.

What's a volcano's favorite song?

"Lava Nagila"

How do weight lifters congratulate each other?

"Muscle tov!"

What did the boy say when he dropped the scrolls?

"What a mess-uzah!"

Knock, knock.

Who's there?

Bupkis.

Bupkis who?

Bupkis I said so!

What do you get when you cross poison ivy with the Bible?

A midrash

What did the socks say to the kippah?

"You go on ahead. I'll follow you on foot!"

What do you call a Jewish crustacean?

A crab-bi

Why is it always hot in a hora circle?

Because a circle is 360 degrees

Knock, knock.

Who's there?

Levi.

Levi who?

Leave? I just got here.

What do you call a yarmulke you wear on your knee?

A kneecap

What did one centipede say to the other during the hora?

"You're stepping on my foot, my foot, my foot, my foot, my foot . . ."

Ricki: My family always celebrates Yom Kippur with a fast.

Romi: We do, too! The faster we eat, the more food we get.

What do dogs do at age 13?

They have a Bark Mitzvah.

What kind of dance do Hebrew school teachers like best?

Attendance

A rabbi was asked why Jews always answer a question with another question. "Why not?" he said.

What currency do Jewish ogres use?

Shrek-els

Why can't an octopus dance the hora?

There aren't enough people to hold his hands.

What do sheep wear to temple?

Yarn-ulkes

At what point does a lamb become a sheep?

When it has had its Baaaaa *Mitzvah*

Gideon: Did you hear the joke about the Jewish circle dance?

Naama: No, what is it?

Gideon: Never mind, it's hora-ble.

Gabriela: Look, Mom. I finally finished the puzzle!

Mom: Puzzle tov!

Why did the rabbi invite the vegetable band to play for the hora?

Because it had a good beet

How do chickens dance the hora?

Chick to chick

What do Jewish moose hang on their doors?

Moose-uzahs

What do you call steaks ordered by ten Jews?

Filet minyan

How do shellfish say congratulations?

"Mussel tov!"

What do cars do at age 13?

They have a Car Mitzvah.

Why don't dogs dance the hora?

They have two left feet.

How did the Jewish soccer player get hurt?

He Torah ligament!

Noah's son walks into a kosher deli and orders a sandwich.

"Sorry," said the clerk. "We don't serve Ham."

Where did the dinosaur have its Bar Mitzvah?

Jew-rassic Park

Where do yarmulkes get made?

Manhattan

A rabbi walked into a synagogue. "Ouch!" he said.

Knock, knock.

Who's there?

Judea.

Judea who?

Don't Judea leave without taking leftovers home!

Nina: Did you see the robot doing the hora?

Miles: He was a dancing machine!

Why can't you take a picture of a man with a yarmulke?

Because you can't take a picture with a yarmulke

How do hummingbirds sing "Hava Nagila"?

They just hum along because they don't know the words.

What type of dances do Hebrew schools have?

Matzo Balls

Knock, knock.

Who's there?

Judith.

Judith who?

Judith thought these jokes would get old, but they don't!